ILLUSTRATED BACKPACKING AND HIKING DICTIONARY FOR YOUNG PEOPLE

BY RANDY LARSON
ILLUSTRATED BY
ERIC LURIO

PRENTICE - HALL, INC.
Englewood Cliffs, New Jersey

This book is dedicated to my father and stepmother.

Much thanks to Peggy Purvis for typing and reviewing the final manuscript.

*Illustrated Backpacking and Hiking Dictionary
for Young People*
by Randy Larson
Text copyright © 1981
by R. Bartkowech
Illustrations copyright © 1981
by Harvey House, Publishers
Treehouse Paperback edition published 1981 by Prentice-Hall, Inc. by arrangement with Harvey House, Publishers

Printed in the United States of America • J
10 9 8 7 6 5 4 3 2 1

Library of Congress Cataloging in Publication Data
Larson, Randy, 1950-
*Illustrated backpacking and hiking dictionary
for young people.*
Summary: An illustrated dictionary guide to the sports of backpacking and hiking.
1. Backpacking—Dictionaries, Juvenile.
2. Hiking—Dictionaries, Juvenile. [1. Backpacking—Dictionaries. 2. Hiking—Dictionaries]
I. Lurio, Eric. II. Title.
GV199.6.L38 1981 796.5′1′03 81-1942
ISBN 0-13-450759-2 (pbk.) AACR2

FOREWORD

Backpacking is enjoyed the world over by young and old alike, boys and girls and even (when rules and regulations permit) pets. Back country facilities are being used by millions of backpackers, more now than ever before. The word is out! Taking to the hills is good, clean fun. It's also a great way to get a new look at our planet and the things living on it.

Why do so many people love this sport? Why has it become so popular? Besides being just plain *fun,* backpacking is good exercise. Backpacking brings you closer to nature, clean air and spectacular scenery. Backpackers will often tell you they do it for the adventure. They feel fulfilled as they meet the challenges of the weather, their own hopes and the limits of their knowledge. Many love exploring and have interests in sciences like botany, biology and meteorology. Last but not least, this sport can be a great *leisure* activity. You can *relax.* Sit by a waterfall. Watch mountain clouds drifting over a crystal lake.

Before you go off into the wilderness, you'll need to know some basic facts about camping, safety and backpacking. You'll also need some means of transportation to and from the trails. Make *certain* you are physically capable of doing what you plan. Reasonable cooperation from the weather also helps.

For many people, backpacking is part of other fun sports such as bicycle touring, cross-country skiing and mountain climbing. These related sports require special skills and knowledge, so if you are interested in them, learn about them *first,* try them later.

Backpacking has some recent problems. The backwoods environment must be preserved, even while the land is made available to backpackers. Overpopulation in campsites and over-use of trails create maintenance and safety problems. Exploring the wilderness is not much fun under these circumstances. We must make sure that we do not misuse our precious back country. We must not break rules or act without caution, care or common sense.

There are national parks and forests all across the United States and Canada which are open to backpackers. Federal wilderness areas are also ours to use. Mountain ranges all over the world have trails to explore. Also, numerous state parks and local woodland areas allow camping and hiking.

This dictionary covers the many aspects of the exciting sport of backpacking. On the following pages you will soon begin perhaps your first hike: a stroll through the terms, expressions and facts important to today's backpacker. Let's go!

A

Accessories — materials that increase the potential use of your equipment or supplies.

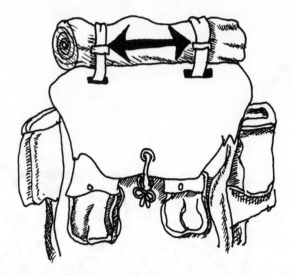

Accessory straps — straps used to attach your sleeping bag and other loads to your pack. They are made of leather, cloth, nylon, canvas or other materials. These straps can be used to add pockets to the outside of your pack or to tighten down equipment so nothing flops around.

Adhesive tape — white tape, sticky on one side, used for many first aid purposes. It also comes in handy to patch torn tents or bags.

Adventure — an experience in which you don't know exactly what is going to happen.

A-frame — a tent or other shelter constructed so that the front and back walls are shaped like a capital *A*. It has sloping sides (a sloping roof) and is sturdy under most conditions.

Air mattress — an air-filled mattress used under a sleeping bag as a cushion and for insulation. It is not a good choice because it does not insulate very well. If you spring a leak you'll have no cushion either. A better bet is a foam pad.

Altitude — a measurement of how high you are above sea level. Will you be camping on a beach or high in the mountains? Plan ahead. At higher altitudes your cooking time will be longer. This means you will need to bring more fuel. Be in good physical condition if you plan to hike far at very high altitudes.

Antiseptic — a substance used on cuts, burns and blisters to clean and to prevent infection. After using antiseptic, protect the area and keep it clean by applying a bandage, tape, moleskin, etc.

Axe — a sharp tool with a handle and blade. An axe used in backpacking is small and lightweight. It comes in handy for gathering fuel, making stakes or clearing a way out if you fall into a briar patch!

B

Back country — areas of forest or mountains which take some effort to reach. If you plan on hiking deep into the back country, you should have maps and other navigational equipment and know how to use them.

Backpack — to go backpacking. Also, a sack or bag worn on your back to carry equipment and supplies. Backpacks are usually made of canvas, leather or rugged synthetic materials. Some have an internal frame, others an external frame. They often have outside pockets. Inside the main compartment, dividers are sometimes used for easier storage of specific items. There are backpacks made for carrying loads of almost all sizes and weights. Some backpacks are made for special purposes like mountain climbing, cross-country skiing or bicycle touring. Know what you are buying and what you need the pack for. It will be your central piece of equipment and your portable home.

Backpacker — a person who goes backpacking. You! Me! Us!

Backpacking — the sport of hiking off into the woods with enough supplies on your back and enough "smarts" in your head to stay alive, have fun, relax, explore, etc.

Backtracking — a method used to try to find out how you lost the path. Retrace your steps. Go back to the last place where you knew where you were.

Backwoods — lots of trees? No houses around for miles? No fields of corn or potatoes? You are probably off in the backwoods. See *back country*.

Backwoodsmen — men who live in or grew up in the backwoods. Backwoodswomen too!

Bag — a sack used to carry supplies: a backpack, stuff sack, tent sack, etc.

Balaklava — a combination of hat and scarf. Balaklavas are excellent for keeping your head warm and preserving body heat.

Bandanna — a loose, lightweight scarf worn around the neck to prevent sunburn at high altitudes or in the desert.

Bathroom — a necessity of life. Dig a hole about one foot deep on high ground and far from any streams, rivers or lakes. Fill the hole with a little dirt after each use. When you leave the area, fill the hole completely and cover it over with brush, twigs, etc.

Bats — mammals with wings. They fly around at dusk and at night and sleep in caves. If you are near bats, don't panic. They are very interesting to watch! Wear a hat or hair net. If a bat gets tangled in your hair, it's haircut time!

Bears — bears are not furry toys to be cuddled. You can watch them from a safe distance, but *never feed the bears*. Animals in the wild can be very dangerous. In bear country store your food far from your tent. If bears do come for your food, let them take it!

Beaver — a rodent best known for building dams. Dusk is the best time to watch beavers building or repairing a dam. Remember, wild animals are unpredictable and can be dangerous, so keep a safe distance. Use binoculars!

Belt pack — a tiny pack, about the size of a pocket, which can be attached to your belt. Belt packs can be used for carrying first aid or other supplies during short hikes from camp.

Bicycle touring — a fast-growing sport combining bicycling and backpacking. It requires basic knowledge of backpacking and of the bicycle, related equipment and cycling experience. Cyclists are able to cover much greater distances in far less time than hikers. Bicycle touring is usually enjoyed for traveling and seeing local sights or the whole country. It can also get you from home to the trail head or from one distant trail or campsite to another. Bike routes on state and country roads have been set up all across the U.S. and in parts of Canada.

Binoculars — an instrument that lets you see far away scenes "up close." Watch bears and deer safely and without disturbing their natural activities. Watch a rare bird nesting way up in the trees or on a cliff ledge. With skill, you can even take pictures through binoculars with a camera. Use binoculars to scout out your surroundings and to examine what is coming up on your hike. Also called "field glasses."

Biodegradable — something that will decompose into harmless materials that will not pollute the land or water. All your cleaning solutions, soap and even toothpaste should be biodegradable. The rule is: if anything you will carry into the woods is available in biodegradable form, buy it that way.

Biology — the study of life. The study of all living things and how their systems function as they stay alive. An interest and love of animals, plants and (yes!) even insects calls many of us into the back country. Backpacking can lead you into the woods, and you might come out so interested in the science of life that you become a biologist!

Bird watching — the hobby and science of observing birds in their natural environment. Binoculars and an identification book are great bird watching aids. Make notes of flight patterns, where each species likes to nest and any unusual habits. Keep your ears open for those beautiful songs, for if there is bird *watching,* there is bird *listening* too!

Blister — a spot of swollen skin caused by friction or burning. Friction from your boot can cause a "hot spot" on your foot. If you catch a "hot spot" early enough, you can cover it with a bandage and perhaps avoid a painful blister. If you do get a blister, put antiseptic on it. Then cushion it with moleskin and tape over the moleskin.

Body heat — the natural heat of your body. In cold weather body heat must not be allowed to escape. Warm clothing is important, especially gloves and a hat. If weather conditions become extreme, find shelter.

Boiling — the easiest and most efficient method of cooking in the woods. When water reaches its boiling point it is hot enough to cook your food or make your soup. Remember, your altitude will affect the boiling point. The amount of time it takes to cook your food will depend on whether you are way up in the clouds or down in the sand dunes. See *boiling point.*

Boiling point — the temperature at which your cooking water starts to bubble and slowly change into steam. Water takes longer to boil at higher elevations because the pressure of the atmosphere is less.

Bonfire — a big fire that looks pretty but wastes fuel and can cause ecological damage. To stay warm you should rely on the right clothes and shelter. A large fire built for heat should only be needed under extremely cold conditions.

Booties — outdoor slippers! Soft, cushioned boots lined with down or other filler to keep tired feet warm and comfy after a long hike! They're not a necessity, but they're fun to have.

21

Boots — footwear worn on hikes over long distances and when carrying heavy loads. Boots supply greater support for your feet than regular shoes, and they keep you warmer and drier. Boots are made in many weights and designs. Choose the right boots for your purpose. Check the sole, the construction and the flexibility. New boots should fit snugly, but they should not feel tight. They should *not* hurt. If a salesperson tells you new boots *always* hurt, you're in the wrong store! Say bye-bye with a smile, and take your business elsewhere.

Botany — the science which studies plant life. Many beautiful wildflowers grow in the backwoods, but some are very rare, so *please* don't pick them! Study the vegetation, and how it gets water. Note where certain plants and flowers grow best. Know which plants are poisonous. Learning about herbs and edible plants can be fun and can come in very handy if a bear eats all your food!

Breaking trail — leaving the established trails and making a trail of your own. This can be dangerous if you are not careful. Breaking trail is against the rules in many national forests so read the regulations before you take to the hills!

Breathable — a material or container which does not completely trap air in (or completely keep air out) is called "breathable." This term also refers to the quality of the air itself. If you climb too high in the mountains and the oxygen gets too thin, the air is not breathable. Then again, the air down here in some of our cities is not very breathable either!

Butane — a liquid cooking fuel kept under low pressure in a metal cartridge, used with a small, portable butane cook-stove. The flame from butane is clean and easy to work with. Take the empty fuel cartridges with you when you leave the woods.

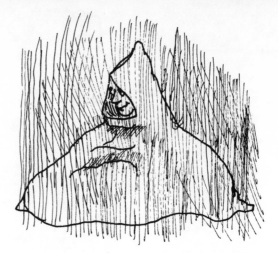

C

Cagoule — a long, one-piece rain suit which has a hood and is open on the bottom. If you sit down and pull your feet up into it, you will be almost completely protected from the rain. A drawstring around the bottom hem can be pulled tight to seal you in.

Calories — food stores energy. When you eat food, the energy is transferred into heat (calories) which gives your body energy and the ability to keep warm.

Camp — your tent set up nice and sturdy (we hope!), your fire established safely and efficiently, and the surrounding area necessary to support your camping activities.

Campfire — the fire you build in your camp.

Camping — the activities involved in setting up and maintaining a camp. Camping also means "backpacking." "Let's go camping!" does not simply mean, "Let's go set up a camp!"

Camping permit — a permit (usually a signed piece of paper) which states that you are allowed to camp in the area mentioned on the permit. Many areas require that you have a permit before setting up camp, so check the rules with a ranger or park official.

Campsite — the place where you choose to set up your camp. A clearing in the woods makes a good site. Dry, level ground is best. Find a site early enough so you are not left stumbling around in the dark. In some areas, you are allowed to set up only at established campsites, so check first.

Canadian National Parks Bureau — write to this agency in Ottawa, Canada for rules, regulations and other information about backpacking through Canada.

Canteen — a container used to carry your water supply into the woods. Canteens and water bottles are available in many styles and price ranges. Choose the one best suited to your needs.

Canvas — a sturdy, tightly woven material made from material fibers. Canvas is used to make backpacks and tents. Most packs are no longer made out of canvas because materials that are lighter and more water-resistant are available.

Capability — the physical and emotional strength and knowledge you need to complete a task or goal. Plan your hike and your outing within the reaches of your capability. Be smart enough to know when you have bitten off more than you can chew. Tomorrow's another day!

Caves — holes in the sides of mountains or hills. Many are large enough to walk in. If you are careful, exploring a cave with an expert is exciting and rewarding. Do not *play* in caves. If a storm is coming your way, do not hide in a cave. Lightning tends to strike at cave entrances.

Challenge — something you attempt to do even though you are not certain you can succeed. Backpacking is a challenge because you don't know how well you can do until you try.

☐ TENT
☐ TV
☐ BEER
☐ POTATO
☐ CHIPS

Check list — a list of what you want to take into the woods. The list helps you organize your equipment and supplies. When you first pack everything, check each item off the list. Before you begin to hike into the woods, make one final check at the trail head.

Chipmunks — striped rodents that look like tiny squirrels. They're cute, but remember, they *are* wild. These little critters run so fast you can go cross-eyed trying to watch their crazy hopping-around. Chipmunks get bold sometimes and stop to pose for pictures.

Cleaning up — if you wash your clothes, let them dry in the wind and sun. Never wash dirty dishes in the waterways. Clean them with a plastic scrub pad and biodegradable soap, *then* rinse them.

Climate — the weather in any area of the country, or in areas like mountain ranges, deserts or beaches. A description of the climate of an area would include the temperature and any wind, rain, snow or sleet to be reported. Don't plan your first hike in a climate like the North Pole's!

Clothing — what you wear should be appropriate to the climate, the season and the specific weather conditions. All clothing should be considered carefully, from under-clothes, socks, pants and shirts, to outerwear and boots. Learn about down jackets, rain gear, summer hiking clothes, and don't leave out a swim suit — just in case!

Coat — your heaviest piece of outerwear. A full-length coat is, of course, too clumsy to do much hiking in, but a down coat covering you from your shoulders to just above the knees is sometimes necessary if the weather you expect will be extreme.

Cold — if, every time you breathe, your breath instantly freezes into a solid cone of ice and falls to the path in front of you, it's cold out! If you do not dress well enough to help your body maintain its normal temperature (98.6°F), you will *feel* cold!

Collapsible water bucket — a lightweight, plastic water bucket which collapses to a very small size when not in use. Water should be kept near your campfire in case of emergencies, but you don't want to have to use your *drinking water* unless absolutely necessary. The solution: a collapsible water bucket which can transport water from a nearby stream, river or lake.

Compass — a device that helps hikers find the direction they want to travel in. A magnetized needle points to the north magnetic pole. If your maps indicate that you should be hiking "due south" (directly south), then you need to walk in the direction opposite to which your compass needle is pointing. A compass is a must when hiking into the back country. You can also use your watch as a compass:

    1. Point the hour hand at the sun.

    2. Imagine a line drawn from the center of the watch through a point on the edge of the watch which is halfway between the hour hand and the number 12.

    3. This imaginary line points "due south," but use standard time only (compensate for daylight saving time).

Condensation — the formation of liquid from vapor. If your tent material is waterproof, it will not be able to "breathe." Water vapor will condense (form water droplets), and these droplets will cling to the inside of the tent until, just after you get to sleep, they will drip down onto your face! Tent material (except for the floor) should be water repellent, not waterproof.

Conservation — all the activities and procedures involved in preserving a supply of something.

Conserve — to maintain a supply of something for as long as you can, by using only what you need, and sometimes by trying to make do with less than you're used to.

Construction — the way something is put together. Construction of a pack or tent will affect how it is used. Construction of your boots will affect how they feel and how long they'll last.

32

Cooking — food should be cooked in such a way as to conserve fuel and, of course, make the food tasty! Some pre-packed foods require special preparation before you cook them, so read the package. Learn how to cook over an open fire or with a cook-stove. Boiling and frying are the two easiest cooking methods when you are out camping.

Cooking fire — an open fire built to cook food. Make sure there is nothing which can catch fire around the spot you choose. You can also dig a fire pit. A good fire conserves fuel, is easy to control and produces a steady, hot flame with little or no smoke. Remember, open fires are against the rules in some areas.

Cook-stove — a small, portable stove used for cooking. These stoves use white gas, propane, kerosene or butane for fuel. Cook-stoves can be very dangerous if you don't know what you are doing.

Cot — a bed made with material stretched in a collapsible frame. Cots are too bulky and heavy to bring backpacking. They are also inefficient, because your body heat escapes into the air between the cot and the ground.

Cotton — a natural material made from the fiber of the cotton plant. Blended with wool, this fabric makes very suitable backpacking clothes.

Cross-country — a great distance, or the distance equal to going across the entire country.

Cross-country skiing — a sport in which skiers use special backpacking equipment and skis to cover large distances over snow.

D

Day-hike — a short hike into the woods or away from the campsite which has you back by sunset.

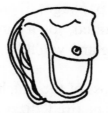

Day-pack — a small, lightweight pack which has no internal or external frame. Use a day pack to carry what you need on a day-hike. Bicyclists use day-packs to carry books or a change of clothes.

Day-trip — a complete backpacking or hiking trip done in one day. You can carry less equipment because you don't need your tent.

Deer — beautiful animals which usually graze quietly in meadows or on mountain foothills. If a pack of deer happen to be running in your direction, jump behind a tree and let them pass. Don't try to out-run them. They're probably more scared than you are, and they'll run faster!

35

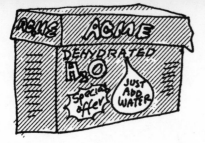

Dehydrated — with all water taken out. Dehydrated foods are lightweight, easy to store, and they don't spoil. Follow cooking instructions on package. If your body is becoming dehydrated, you'll know it because you'll be sweating and you'll be thirsty!

Dehydration — loss of too much water from your body. You'll be tired, dizzy and perhaps have cramps. To prevent dehydration, drink enough liquids and eat foods which have some salt and fat.

Desert — an area of land which has little or no vegetation, the result of low rainfall, extreme winds, or the movement of huge glaciers over the surface. Deserts have lots of sand, some cactus and plenty of *hot* sun. Special know-how is required for camping or hiking in deserts.

Design — the way something looks as a result of construction. The design of quality back-packing equipment is linked primarily to the equipment's *function,* not just its good looks. A pretty tent that can't stand up is pretty irritating!

Dew — natural condensation of water in the atmosphere. Water droplets form on the grass and on plants and on just about anything left outside your tent. Early morning is when we usually find everything covered with dew.

Digestible — food which is easily changed into energy by your body. Don't bring food which is difficult to digest on a hike.

Direction — a key element in navigation. Imagine a line pointing to some fixed point in the distance which you're walking toward; this line indicates your direction. Also, the way your compass needle points: due west, due south, and so on.

Distance and speed — start off your hike at a slow pace. Your speed will pick up naturally as you go, until you reach your most comfortable stride. The kind of terrain you're hiking over and the physical condition of your body will affect the distance you can cover and how long your hike will take. Make a reasonable prediction of the distance you can cover and your speed before you set out. Allow for unknown obstacles.

Distress call — a signal for help. Three of anything is the standard way to signal to others that you need help. Three short blasts on your whistle. Three small signal fires on top of a hill at night.

EASY   MODERATE   ROUGH

Distribution of weight — the weight of your body, your pack and the combined unit of body-and-pack must be distributed evenly for safe hiking. When loading your pack, heaviest items should go close to your back, as far forward as possible. If the terrain is very rugged, heavy items go forward and at the bottom. Moderately rough trails call for most of the weight forward and halfway up the pack. On easy hikes put the weight forward and near the top.

Down filler — down filler is made from the feathers of geese or ducks. Down has many advantages: it keeps you very warm and is *very* lightweight. One problem with down is that if it gets wet, it loses its ability to keep you warm. Under some conditions, synthetic fillers may be better.

39

Downhill hiking — care must be taken when hiking downhill. Do not let gravity get you going too fast for your own safety and the safety of others: your equipment could shake loose and you could injure your feet, ankles and knees.

Dried fruit — an excellent trail snack! Tastes great, gives you energy and it's easy to carry. It's a real treat when mixed with nuts. Dried fruit can also spice up hot cereal on a cold morning.

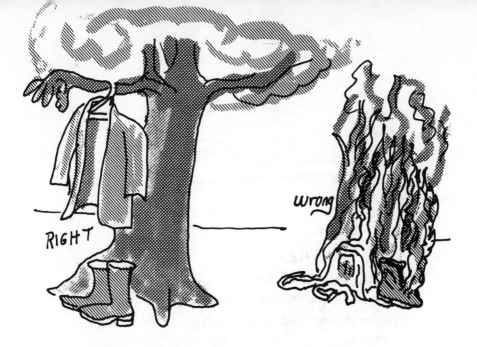

RIGHT

wrong

Drying out — a fire should not be used for drying wet articles. The heat can melt tent or bag materials, warp and crack leather and burn wool. Let your wet boots dry naturally in the shade. Dry wet equipment or other clothing in the sun and wind.

Duff — decayed leaves, branches, twigs, pine cones and grass. Duff often covers a forest floor and makes a soft floor for your tent or sleeping area.

E

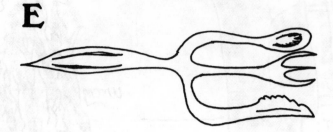

Eating utensils — basic eating utensils include a fork, a knife and a spoon. A spatula can come in handy for cooking. Never bring plastic utensils on a backpacking trip. They crack and break in cold weather, and they're hard to clean. Utensil sets are available which include a spoon, fork and knife.

Ecology — a science which studies the balance between an environment and the creatures which live in it. If you are ecological, you do things which respect this balance.

The elements — the forces which make up the weather: sun, wind, rain, snow, sleet, and so on.

Emergency — a situation in which someone or something needs immediate aid, without which they will suffer harm.

Endangered — someone or something that is in danger. An endangered species is a species close to becoming extinct. Any endangered person or animal you can help *without endangering yourself,* try to help.

Energy — the ability to do work. When energy is used, heat is given off. When your body uses energy it gives off heat: you replace this energy by adding fuel (eating food). When your campfire uses energy, it also gives off heat: you replace its energy by adding fuel (wood). Conserving energy is a good idea, and is sometimes absolutely necessary.

Entomology — the science which studies insects: their bodies, their habits and their habitats (environments). Many who are interested in entomology find backpacking an excellent way to study insects.

44

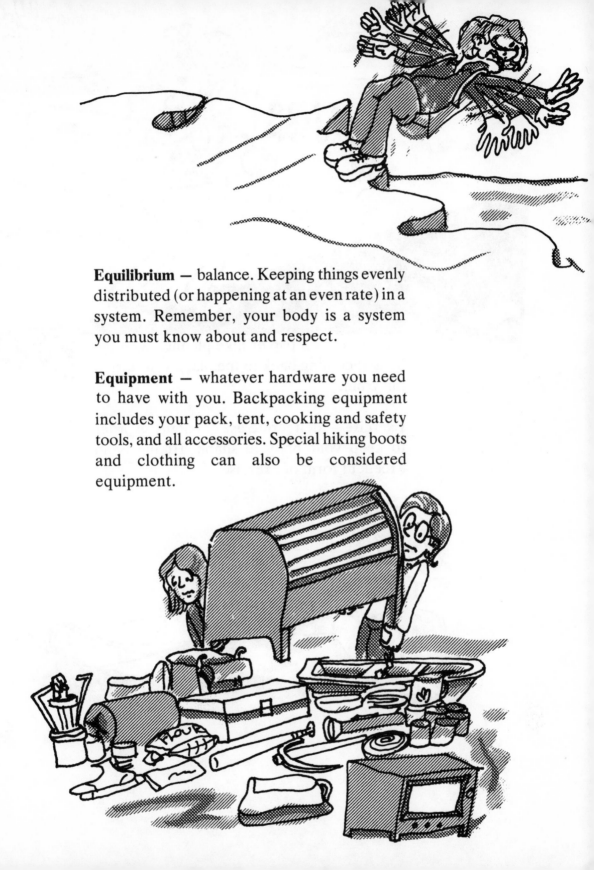

Equilibrium — balance. Keeping things evenly distributed (or happening at an even rate) in a system. Remember, your body is a system you must know about and respect.

Equipment — whatever hardware you need to have with you. Backpacking equipment includes your pack, tent, cooking and safety tools, and all accessories. Special hiking boots and clothing can also be considered equipment.

Excursion — a trip or hike planned with the idea of coming back to the place you started out from.

Exercise — deliberate use of energy in order to keep your body in shape. Hiking is an excellent form of exercise.

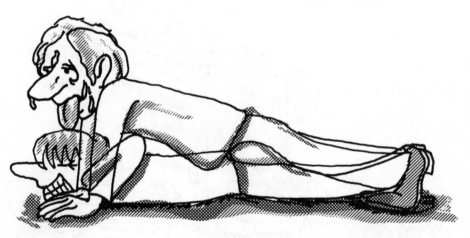

Expedition — a large-scale outing, planned and prepared with the purpose of attaining some goal.

Exploit — to take unfair advantage of something, to use something to an unfair extent, or to exhaust the supply of something. Clean water, fresh air and undeveloped land are some of the natural resources backpackers use and must preserve.

Exploration — the activity of investigating something either for the challenge and adventure, the knowledge you hope to gain, or simply for the fun of it.

Explosive — capable of blowing up! Careful!

Exposure — see *hypothermia.*

External frame — a rigid structure outside the backpack, usually made of aluminum, to which the pack is attached for support.

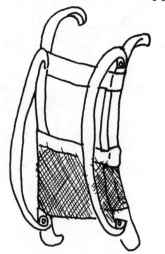

F

Fabrics — materials which are woven, spun, knitted, pressed or produced by other means. Fabrics are used to make your tent, your bags and your clothing. Fabrics used in making backpacking equipment and supplies include wool, canvas, cotton, leather, nylon and other synthetics.

Facilities — things provided to serve a particular purpose. Camping facilities can be anything from a water-supply hookup or bathrooms, to simply an established fire site. If facilities are available, find out what they *are*.

Filler — the material used in lining sleeping bags, jackets, mittens and other items. The purpose of filler is to keep you dry and warm. Down is the most popular, but also the most expensive. Many synthetics (*Polarguard* for one) are quite good. Other synthetics are just junk! Ask around before you count on an unknown filler to keep out the cold.

Fines — penalties for breaking rules. Many parks and forest areas impose strict and costly fines. Some of the heaviest fines are for leaving a fire which is not completely out. If you cause a forest fire, you may have to pay for all damages including fire-fighting, clean-up and loss of land. If you burn down a forest, you'll be paying for a long time. You will also have robbed us all of a forest and taken away the homes of many animals.

Fire hazard — an estimate of how easily a forest could catch fire due to dry weather conditions. Most national parks, forests and wilderness areas post the fire hazard for their area either on a bulletin board, or on a special sign which will read: "FOREST FIRE DANGER TODAY" with an arrow pointing to "Moderate," "High," or "Extreme." Be careful with fire.

Fire permit — a signed piece of paper which allows you to build a campfire in the area mentioned on the permit. Any restrictions as to what sort of fire you can build or where you can build it should be written on the permit. Many areas require you to have a fire permit to build a fire; without it you'll get a fine.

Fire pit — a hole dug in the ground, in which you build your campfire. Make sure to cut and remove any tree roots because the fire can sometimes travel underground along the roots and pop up somewhere else. When you're ready to leave, fill the pit in, put back any rocks you moved and re-landscape the area.

Fire ribbon — a jellied fuel kept in a squeeze tube. It's excellent for starting a fire in snow or light rain. A fire ribbon is also very helpful in getting damp wood to "take a flame."

Fire ring — a ring of rocks which form a circle around a campfire. The rocks act as a windbreak for the fire and they also generate heat. When you put out the fire, don't throw cold water on the hot rocks. They might explode! Be sure you don't leave behind any hot rocks which might start a fire.

Fire site — the place you choose to put your campfire. Keep the fire far from tents and equipment so flying embers don't burn holes in the material. Choose level ground. Make sure you build the fire on a surface which cannot burn or smolder.

First aid — the methods, medicines, equipment and procedures used in the immediate treatment of an illness or injury. Learn the basics of first aid before you go hiking.

First aid kit — an easily stored kit containing a first aid manual and the basic medicines and equipment necessary to give first aid.

Fishing — one fun way to get some tasty backwoods food. Bring a lightweight, collapsible pole. If the pole has a reel, carry it separately. Check any rules or regulations for fishing in your camping area. Do you need a permit?

Fly — one of the bugs which bug us, even when eating around a campfire. Up in the mountains there are usually no flies. It's too cool up there for them. Also refers to a tent accessory (see *rainfly).*

Foam pad — a lightweight pad used under your sleeping bag which provides a cushion and insulates you from the cold ground.

Food — anything you eat which provides your body with energy and nutrition. Food you carry when you go hiking must be lightweight and easy to prepare. It must not spoil easily. Your foods should include sources of protein, fat, starch, salt, water and honey (or sugar). Some favorite backpacking foods are powdered eggs and milk, noodles, cereals, meat bars and dehydrated soups, vegetables and fruits.

Foot care — foot care includes wearing quality, well-fitting boots which provide good support. Wear clean, dry socks. If you feel any pain in your feet, stop and check it. A pebble in your boot? Foot powder on feet and socks is sometimes helpful. Take care of any blisters or "hot spots" right away. See *blister* and *hot spot*.

Footwear — backpacking footwear includes wool socks, hiking boots and sometimes booties or moccasins.

Forest — a large area of land covered with many trees and other plants.

Forester — an officer who works to control and protect a forest area. Foresters can give you information about the sights in the area and any rules or regulations you should know. Also called "forest ranger" or "ranger."

Foul weather gear — clothing specially designed to protect you in extreme weather conditions. Also, a thick, one-piece rain suit.

Frame — any rigid structure which provides support. Tents and backpacks have frames. See *external frame, internal frame* and *tent.*

Freeze-dried — foods which are frozen and dried very quickly in order to preserve them for long periods of time. Perfect for backpacking, these foods are greatly reduced in size, are lightweight and retain their nutritional value.

Friction — the rubbing of two surfaces against one another. This rubbing creates heat. If your boot doesn't fit quite right and part of your foot is constantly rubbing against it as you walk, the heat and abrasion will result in a blister. See *blister.*

Frigid — extremely cold.

Frontier — the border of a large stretch of undeveloped land. Also, the entire undeveloped area.

Fuel bottle — a bottle used to store and carry liquid or gas fuels for your cook-stove. Fuel bottles or cartridges should be carried in an outside pocket of the backpack. This will keep fumes from your food and clothes. See also *fuel cartridge.*

Fuel cartridge — a bottle or other container for storing and carrying cook-stove fuel. It is called a fuel *cartridge* because it is attached directly onto the stove for a continuous fuel supply until the cartridge is used up. Some fuel cartridges can be turned off so you can use only the amount you need. Some cheaper fuel cartridges must be completely used up once attached. Don't leave empty fuel cartridges in the woods!

G

Games — some favorite campfire games include "Simon Says," pantomime, riddles, jokes, impersonations and telling "chain stories." Bring a small, lightweight chess or checker set or a deck of cards for tent games in bad weather.

Garbage — waste left over from consuming food or fuel or anything thrown away. Garbage is every backpacker's responsibility. Do *not* bury your garbage. Pack out all garbage even if it isn't *yours*.

Gear — any equipment or supplies used for a specific purpose such as backpacking, mountain climbing, bicycle touring, cross-country skiing and so on.

Geography — the physical formations and other features of the earth. Geography is obviously of interest to backpackers and all hikers.

Geology — the study of the earth's structure, how the earth was formed and what it has been doing since its birth. Those interested in studying rock formations often become avid backpackers.

AMERICA→ TASTY STRAWBERRY LAYER   CREAMY VANILLA CENTER   YUMMY CHOCOLATE LAYER   ←CHINA

Goose down — a filler made from goose feathers. The best down.

Ground sheet — a sheet of waterproof material used under a tent or sleeping bag to prevent moisture damage and to keep people from getting wet when they go to bed.

Grub — see *food*.

Guide — a person who knows the way to get somewhere or who is familiar with the area. A guide takes charge of leading you in the right direction. Some areas are dangerous or confusing and you *need* a guide.

Guidebook — a book or manual used to get you where you want to go, and to keep you from getting lost. If the area you will hike in has many complicated trails and trail crossings, ask a ranger or park official if a guidebook is available.

Guy ropes — support ropes used with a tent frame to hold the tent steady in wind and form it to its proper shape. Guy ropes should be *tight* when you're done setting up the tent. See *stakes*.

H

Heat — a form of energy produced by a source which loses some of its fuel or mass in the process. Your body produces heat and loses some of its body fat. Your campfire produces heat and uses up its fuel (wood) as it burns. Conserve body heat by dressing warmly. Conserve the heat of your fire by making a fire ring around it. See *fire ring*.

Herbs — plants used for seasoning, as teas, or as medicine. Many have beautiful, sweet smells. Many people who collect, study and use herbs (herbalists) enjoy backpacking as a means of reaching areas where wild herbs grow.

Hide — skin. Animal hides used to be the only material for making packs, straps, tents, blankets, etc. Now we use many synthetic materials or materials made from plants.

Hiker — a person who hikes.

Hiking — evenly-paced walking. People hike for exercise and also to get as deep into the woods as they want. Feet should not be lifted too high off the ground. Conserve energy. Breathe evenly, slowly and deeply. See *downhill hiking, uphill hiking, pace* and *stride.*

Hot spot — a warm feeling on your foot or other part of your body caused by friction. A sure sign you'll be getting a blister unless you do something to prevent it. See *blister, foot care* and *friction.*

Hypothermia — a very serious condition in which your body loses the ability to keep itself warm. If you should be lost or injured and waiting for aid, try to stay warm, dry and protected from the wind. Hypothermia can set in at temperatures well above freezing, and it can kill you. Another word for hypothermia is "exposure."

62

I

Impassable — not possible to pass through or over. A trail or passageway which has become blocked or unusable is impassable.

Information — facts used for the purpose of understanding or becoming aware of something. For large excursions or hikes into the back country, you need information about weather, rules and regulations, terrain, dangerous passes, etc.

Insect repellent — a spray or lotion which is applied to skin, clothing or equipment to keep insects away.

Insects — tiny critters which can bug you. It can be interesting to study how they live and how their bodies operate. They have no backbone and there are three sections to each body! Don't set up camp in swampy areas or you'll have more insects around than you care to study. See *entomology.*

Insect screen — a screen, made of lightweight material, built into your sleeping bag or tent, used to prevent or discourage insects from joining you in bed.

Instinct — the unconscious drive which allows animals and insects to complete necessary tasks without necessarily understanding how or why. Also, a "sense" you have about something. Instinct can *sometimes* help you find your way out of the woods, but *don't* rely on it!

Insulation — any material or substance which keeps you warm and the cold *out*! Also, a material or substance which lines a container to keep food or drinks cold.

Internal frame — a rigid structure built into the construction of the backpack, designed for support and to help you maintain your balance when hiking over very rough ground. Mountain climbers use internal frame packs to give themselves a better chance of staying on their feet.

J

Jacket — a short coat, usually covering you from your shoulders to just above the knee or to your waist. Down jackets are warm enough for most cold weather conditions. Materials and designs vary widely. Check the labels, manufacturer's claims and the workmanship before you buy.

Jellied alcohol — a fuel suggested for cooking light meals or making hot drinks. Since it doesn't put out much heat, it's not good for heavy meals. Empty containers must be carried out of the woods when you leave. See *Sterno*.

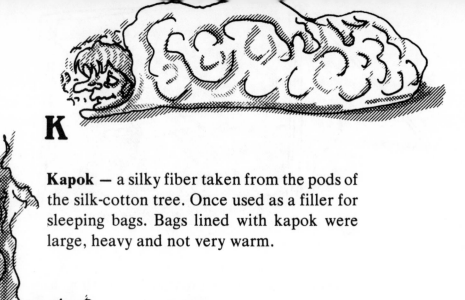

K

Kapok — a silky fiber taken from the pods of the silk-cotton tree. Once used as a filler for sleeping bags. Bags lined with kapok were large, heavy and not very warm.

Kerosene — an oil fuel used in some cookstoves. Stoves using kerosene are not very popular because they are smelly, difficult to get started and there is usually no way to adjust the flame.

Kindling — branches or small pieces of soft, quick-burning wood used in getting your campfire started.

Knapsack — another name for a backpack.

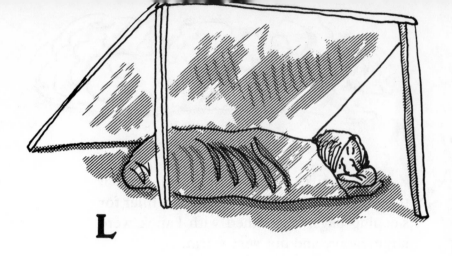

L

Lean-to — a shelter created by slanting a large piece of material in such a way that it acts as a roof and a windbreak. The roof should face into the wind and be slanted enough to cover you and your equipment. A canvas tarp or sheet of heavy nylon works well for this purpose.

Lightning — to avoid being struck by lightning during a storm, *stay clear* of caves, high ground or a tree in the middle of a clearing. Lightning can be very beautiful, but it can also be very dangerous. Lightning can burn victims severely, put them in deep shock, paralyze them or even kill.

Lightweight — anything which does not weigh very much. Weight is a factor which should *always* be considered when buying any backpacking equipment or supplies. Take the most lightweight equipment that will do a good job.

The load — everything you are carrying as you hike. Most of the load will, of course, be on your back (in or on your backpack).

Loading the pack — how you load your pack will partly depend on your pack's design and construction. Your equipment and supplies should be packed neatly, with the weight evenly distributed. Organize the pack so things you use together are near one another. Trail snacks should be in easy-to-get-to side pockets. Don't tie too much to the outside of the pack. Anything outside the pack must be tied down securely. Canteens can go outside. Your sleeping bag should be rolled up, stuffed in its sack and attached with accessory straps below the main body of the pack. Roll up the foam ground pad and ground sheet together and attach them to the frame above the pack. See *equilibrium.*

Lug sole — a hard rubber sole constructed with a deep, cleated design. Lug soles are thick and solid. They are used as the bottoms of good quality hiking boots and give the hiker excellent traction and support when hiking over rugged terrain. *Vibram* soles are the most famous brand of lug soles. (They're well-respected too.)

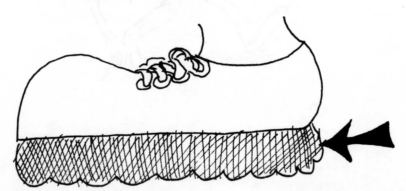

M

Marking location — a procedure used to find out where you are or to find a lost trail or path. Mark the spot you're at (a few crossed pieces of wood or a piece of bright material are good) and then check a short distance away to find the path you wanted to be on. Then *return* to the marker. If you find your path, you should return to your marker and set things back the way they were. If you don't find your path, repeat this procedure using the same marker until all directions have been investigated.

Meat bars — dehydrated bars of meat, shaped and packaged like candy bars. Add these to soups and the meats taste like regular meat (well, almost).

Mess kit — a kit containing cooking equipment. Mess kits usually contain at least pots, cups and bowls. The best kits fold up into one compact unit. Aluminum mess kits are lightest. Be careful not to burn your lips or hands on the hot aluminum. Buy a pot gripper. Mess kits are usually available for one, two or four people.

Meteorology — the study of the weather. An interest in unusual weather conditions and cloud formations has led many a hiker into the sport of backpacking.

Mini-packs — any small or tiny pack. See *belt pack* and *waist pack*.

Moleskin — a soft, protective covering used in first aid for blisters, bruises and other minor injuries. Moleskin is made of a furry cotton material. See *blister*.

Mountain climbing — the sport of climbing up mountains without using trails or paths. This is an *extremely* dangerous sport if you don't know what you are doing. Find a good teacher with lots of experience. Special backpacking equipment and supplies are used in this sport.

Mountain men — trappers, explorers and others who live or spend most of their time in the mountains, especially the frontier people of the past.

Mountain pass — a pathway, often dangerous, over or through a mountain range.

Mountains — spectacular geological formations where the land has buckled up due to tremendous forces within or on the surface of the earth. Mountains are very much larger than hills and are often very steep.

Mummy bag — a sleeping bag designed in the shape of your body. The shape resembles a mummy case. Mummy bags weigh less than rectangular bags because they use less material. They also keep you warmer. See *sleeping bag*.

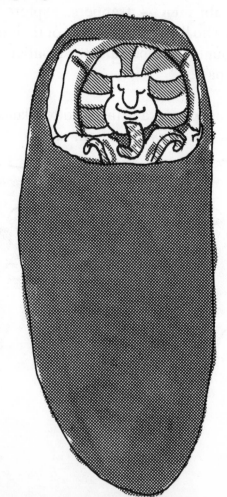

N

National parks and forests — parks and forests protected and controlled by a national government.

Navigation — planning where you are going, figuring out how to get there, and going there. Many tools are used in navigation: compass, trail markers, maps, guidebooks, sun, wind, stars and even your watch. If you are without a clue as to how to navigate (go in the correct direction), then you had better start considering yourself lost. See *orientation.*

Nomad — a person whose way of life involves constantly moving from place to place. "Home is where the tent is," but this is a *rough* way to live.

Nutrition — the process by which a body takes in food and drink to grow and maintain good health.

Nylon — a synthetic fabric used to make packs, sacks, tents and other shelters, groundsheets, etc. Nylon is strong and lightweight. It can be purchased as either water-repellent or waterproof.

O

Open fire — a fire built in the open, either in a pit, surrounded by rocks, or completely exposed. Open fires are used for cooking and sometimes for heat. Depending on the rules for your area, a fire built in a stationary, outdoor fireplace may or may not be considered an open fire.

Opossum — a marsupial (carries its young in a pouch located on its belly). Opossums are most active at night. They used to be seen mostly in Central or South America or Australia, but now they're found in North America too. Opossums look a bit like big rats, but are cuter. Remember, they are wild, unpredictable and sometimes dangerous. Opossums are short-tempered and have a nasty bite. Also called "possum."

Organization — things grouped together in such a way that they can be used safely, efficiently and orderly. Be organized when you load your backpack. Don't just throw everything in any old way or you'll have problems later. "Where's the mess kit?" "You forgot the *food*!?" Also, a group of things or people organized for a particular purpose.

Orientation — knowing where you are. Tools used in orientation include maps, attention to your surroundings and backtracking. See *navigation*.

Outing — another word for an excursion, a backpacking trip or a hike.

Outing report — a report made before or after an outing. It includes your starting and ending locations, trails travelled (or trails you plan to travel), and starting and finishing times and dates (actual or proposed). For any long hike or camping trip, *always* leave word with a park or forest official, or with any responsible person not part of your hiking group, and include the information mentioned above.

78

P

Pace — the speed at which you are hiking. See *stride*.

Pack — a backpack.

Packboard — a backpack and frame combination used until about 1935. The frame consisted of a wooden board with a dowel or thick branch attached to each side. A canvas or cloth pack was wrapped around this frame. These packs were heavy, awkward, and they made your back sweat.

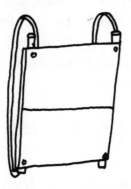

Parka — a jacket which has a hood attached to it. Many parkas provide rain and wind protection. Parkas lined with down are warmest.

Perspiring — see *sweating*.

Pioneers — people who travel into unknown land to settle or explore it. The thrill of exploring and living in unknown areas leads many people to the sport of backpacking.

Pocket knife — a small, lightweight knife, usually with one or two blades. It's always a good idea to have one when backpacking. It has many uses. Make sure the blades are sharp, or it's *useless*.

Poncho — a hooded cloak used for rain protection.

Pot gripper — a tool which keeps your hands from burning on hot pots. It attaches to the edge of the pot to form a cool handle. Usually a spring action controls the clamp. It's a *very* helpful little tool, and a must with an aluminum mess kit.

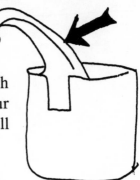

Pour spout — a nozzle which you can attach to your fuel bottle so that when you fill your cook-stove the fuel goes in the stove, not all over the ground.

Powdered food — food which is in the form of powder, usually as a result of being condensed and dehydrated. Powdered food is lightweight and easy to carry. It won't spoil. Powdered eggs and powdered milk are popular. Pancake mix which includes the milk and eggs (just add water!) is a favorite in the back country.

Pre-cooked foods — foods partially or completely cooked before being packaged. Pre-cooked foods save preparation time, especially at higher altitudes. It takes longer to get the water boiling and the food cooked when you're way up there in the clouds.

81

Predictions — statements made in an attempt to accurately describe conditions, events or needs which will occur in the future. Predictions must be made in order to plan an outing. What are the weather predictions? How much food consumption do you predict? (Always bring more food than you predict, *never* less.) How long do you think it will take to get where you want to go? Ask yourself many questions. Make sensible predictions.

Preserve — an area of land protected for people or wildlife. Also, to maintain over a long period of time. Backpacking foods are preserved in a variety of ways: dehydrated, freeze-dried, etc.

Priming fuel — a small amount of fuel used in getting your cook-stove started.

Procedure — a way to do something, or get something accomplished. It often involves steps. It always involves the ability to follow instructions or directions. After you learn a procedure, you do it by memory.

Propane — a fuel used in cook-stoves. It's a bad choice. Fuel cartridges filled with propane are under very high pressure and therefore can be quite dangerous. The empty cartridges are heavy. Go with white gas or butane.

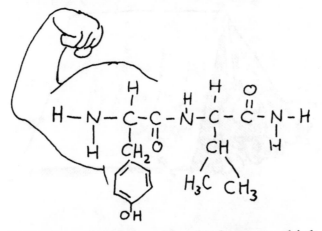

Protein — a nutritional food substance which comes from animal or vegetable foods. Your body needs protein to grow and to be able to heal itself. Protein must always be part of your diet, especially when hiking, camping or doing any regular exercising.

Provisions — another word for "supplies."

Public lands — land open to all of us to use for our enjoyment, as long as we obey the rules and respect all life and the environment. National parks and forests are public lands.

Pup tent — a small A-frame tent for one or two people. Pup tents are a good choice for short outings. They are lightweight and easy to set up.

R

Raccoon — a mammal found in North America. The black markings on its face look like the mask of a bandit. Raccoons are real scavengers. Usually you'll see them feeling through shallow waters with their paws. These critters have perhaps the greatest ability to use their paws of all mammals. This is one reason they are so good at stealing your food. In "coon" country, string your food up and hang it from a tree to keep them from it. Don't scare a mother raccoon when she's out walking her cubs or she'll get mad and hiss and screech.

Rainfly — a waterproof sheet of material which sets up like a cover over your tent. Use it if you're expecting showers. Your tent should come supplied with a rainfly. If it doesn't, ask for one. A rainfly can also be used as a light shelter on clear nights, to keep the morning dew off you.

Rain gear — clothing that provides protection when it's raining, including rain jackets, rain pants and ponchos.

Ranger — see *forester*.

Rations — food taken along on a journey or outing which must be made to last over a certain period of time.

Register — to sign in at a park office and give information about your intended activities. Even if not required, this is always a good idea. See *outing report*.

Repair kit — a small repair kit could include a needle and thread, some strong cord, a small tube of plastic glue and a few bits of material. Mistakes and accidents sometimes happen, and it's a relief to know you can patch your tent or bag before the storm comes in.

Rescue — an attempt made to save someone or something from danger, injury or death. If you get in trouble out in the woods and you are waiting for someone to rescue you, stay put, conserve all your resources, and stay dry and warm. See *distress signal*.

Resources — any supply you use often and rely on. Our natural resources include our air, water, land and anything we pull out of the ground.

Re-usable — something which can be used again, often many times. This makes the product economical and does not waste the natural resources and energy required to make a new one. If any backpacking equipment is available in re-usable form, buy it that way.

Rivers — large waterways which flow in a channel carved out by the force of the water. Be careful when crossing rivers. They are often quick-running and *cold!* Do not throw *anything* in the rivers.

Rope — nylon rope is lightweight and strong. It's a good idea to bring 30 to 40 feet of rope along to help in crossing rivers or streams and for emergencies or repairs.

Route-finding — figuring out which way to go. This can get confusing out in the woods. See *navigation* and *trail markers*.

ROUTE 267C
NEXT EXIT

Rucksack — a backpack, usually the older style, made out of canvas. "Rücken" means "back" in German.

Rules and regulations — guidelines, written or spoken, referring to your conduct and responsibilities. When in any controlled area, always ask about the rules and regulations and *obey* them. If the area is not controlled, act with caution, care and respect for the environment and all its life.

S

Sack — a bag. See *stuff sack.*

Saddle pack — a small pack which fits comfortably on your dog's back. Half the pack hangs on each side of the dog. He or she can carry his/her own bowl, dry food and a lightweight chain. Distribute the weight evenly. Check first if pets are allowed where you're going.

Safety — a way of acting and thinking so that accidents, injuries and damage are prevented. Always be safety conscious when going backpacking.

Safety matches — matches specially prepared to reduce the chance of them igniting accidentally.

Salt — your backpacking diet should include foods which contain salt (unless you're on a low salt diet). This helps replace natural body salts lost through sweating. Under *extreme* conditions, when you're sweating a great deal, it may be advisable to take a salt tablet.

Scout — someone who explores the trails ahead of you and reports back to your party any dangers or obstacles ahead.

Scrub pad — a small, lightweight pad, usually made of coiled strands of plastic, used to scrub dirty pots and pans clean before rinsing.

Shelter — any structure which protects you from the weather or some danger. See *tent*.

Shorts — pants which stop above the knee. A good choice for summer hiking. In very hot sun or high altitudes, it's better to wear long pants or you could get sunburned.

Shoulder straps — straps which come over each shoulder to hold the pack on your back. Straps can be made of leather, canvas or other materials. The thickness and construction of the straps vary with the load capacity, design and construction of each pack.

Signal fire — a fire made to signal for help: a distress fire. In the daytime, signal fires are usually made to send up a thick column of smoke. At night, three small fires on a hillside signal to others that you need help.

Signal mirror — a mirror used to let others know you are in trouble and need aid. Try to make the sun's rays flash off the mirror. Three flashes in each sequence is the signal for help.

Skin lotions — creams applied to the skin to keep insects away or to prevent sunburn (in hot weather or high altitudes) or skin chaffing (in cold or windy weather). Always bring sunburn lotion on your hike.

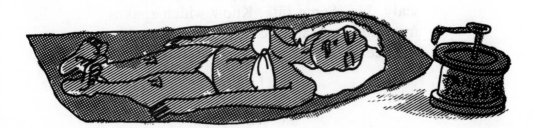

Sleeping bag — a long bag made for sleeping outdoors. The bag should keep you warm and dry. It should be comfortable in warm weather but keep you toasty warm when it gets nippy. The bag can be lined with different kinds of fillers, down or synthetics. The outside material should be water repellent (not water-proof) so you don't sweat like mad when you're zipped up in it. See *filler* and *mummy bag*.

Snake-bite kit — a small kit containing medicine and supplies for first aid should you or any other hiker be bitten by a snake. In areas where poisonous snakes are known to live, bringing this kit is a must.

Snakes — long, skinny, legless reptiles with scaly skin. Some bite. Know which snakes are dangerous: rattlesnakes, water mocassins, etc. See *snake-bite kit*.

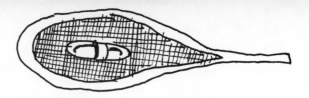

Snowshoes — special shoes (or equipment adapted to boots) designed to make walking on deep snow possible. They sometimes look like tennis rackets for the feet.

Spoilage — anything turning bad due to not being properly preserved. Also, wasting something, using a supply of anything for no good reason.

Squeeze tubes — special containers for food or other liquids or pastes. Squeeze tubes help control how much of the contents come out at once, and where the contents are directed. They look a bit like toothpaste tubes. Many are re-usable.

Stability — the ability to stay on your feet due to even distribution of weight. See *distribution of weight* and *equilibrium*.

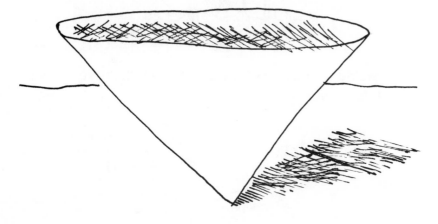

Stakes or spikes — pieces of wood or metal, pointed at one end, which secure guy ropes in the ground so your tent will stay up. See *guy ropes*. Also, any sharp stick stuck into the ground. See *Y-stakes*.

Starch — a necessary part of your backpacking diet. Foods containing starch include potatoes, wheat bread, rice and corn.

Sterno — the most popular brand of jellied alcohol fuel. It comes in a sealed can and is easy to use and clean. Set the can between rocks or in a collapsible sterno stove. Fuel burns right out of the can.

Stride — the size of the steps you take as you hike. See *pace*.

Stuff sack — a bag used to carry and protect a sleeping bag. Also, any bag you stuff something else into for storage.

Sunburn — if you get too much sun, your skin will actually cook. Skin turns red and itchy and is very painful. Too much sun can lead to blisters and even sun poisoning or sunstroke. On hot days or up in high altitudes, cover up. Use a lotion made to protect your skin from burning.

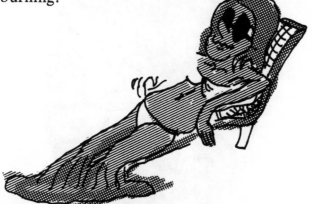

Sunglasses — glasses made with special dark lenses to cut down the amount of the sun's glare that gets into your eyes.

Supplies — those items you must bring which, as you use them, diminish in quantity or quality. The main supplies for backpackers are food, fuel and first aid items.

Surroundings — everything around you in your physical environment. Paying attention to your surroundings can keep you from getting lost.

Sweatband — a piece of absorbent material worn around the forehead to prevent sweat from getting into the eyes. Worn by backpackers during very rugged, lengthy hikes in hot weather.

Sweating — the way your body tries to cool itself off in hot weather. Your body forces some of its water out through the pores (*tiny holes*) of your skin. When you are sweating a lot over a long period of time, keep in mind that you should be replacing the water and salt your body is losing. Eat foods with salt in them. Drink water. Also called "perspiring."

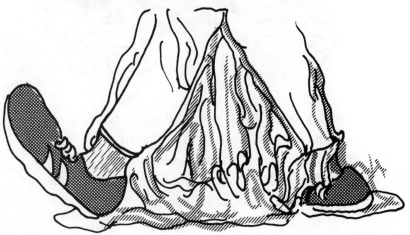

Sweat shirt — a thick, heavy shirt, usually insulated and made of cotton. Sweatshirts come with long or short sleeves.

Swimming — the art, sport and hobby of moving the body on and through the water. When swimming, use the buddy system: *never* swim alone.

Swiss army knife — a medium size knife with many blades and other attachments which fold up into a compact unit. This backpacking tool has dozens of uses. It's better than a single-blade pocket knife.

Switchbacks — trails that make uphill hiking easier. They zigzag back and forth. Switchbacks prevent the soil from wearing away and provide a safer way to get to the top of a hill or mountain.

Synthetic — not made by nature or as the result of natural processes: manmade.

103

T

Tarp — a thick sheet of waterproof nylon or canvas, used as a simple shelter or to protect equipment from weather or curious animals.

Teepee tents — a tent shaped like an Indian teepee, with a single high point, circular base and steeply sloped sides.

Temperature — how hot or cold something is — the air, your body, lake water, your aluminum soup cup — anything. Temperature affects all aspects of your camping trip. For example, the colder the air, the longer it will take for your food to cook and the more fuel you will use.

Tent — your main, overnight shelter. The material should be strong, lightweight and breathable (water repellent). Get a tent which is the right size for your needs. A double wall A-frame is most reliable. Different tents require different set-up techniques, so set your tent up *before* you rely on it out in the woods. Tent accessories should include rainfly, ground-sheet, guy ropes, stakes and insect screen.

105

Tent cover — see *rainfly*.

Tent sack — a stuff sack for your tent. See *stuff sack*.

Tent site — the place where you choose to set up your tent. Your tent site should be on open, level ground with no rocks, pebbles or tree roots. Do not set your tent up near swampy land, dense vegetation, low-lying land, huge rocks or tree limbs. The tent should not be near or downward of your proposed fire site.

Terrain — the structure, shape and make-up of the land. The kind of terrain you'll be hiking on will determine what kind of equipment and supplies you should bring.

Territory — an area of land which has at least one common element, either common location, inhabitation by a certain form of life, or any other unifying factor.

THE BORDERLAND

LOST

NOWHERESVILLE

US

THEM

SOMEBODY ELSE

NEW IMPROVED JERSEY

OCEAN

Thermal underwear — underwear made of a fabric designed to use your body's heat to keep you warm.

Thicket — see *underbrush*.

Ticks — insects with jaws! They don't mind biting into you for a snack! They usually live in or near woods. Check yourself often for ticks when in the mountains or other wooded areas. They thrive in warm weather.

Tinder — very fine twigs, used to start an open fire.

Toilet articles — backpacking toilet articles include washcloth, biodegradable soap, comb, toothbrush and paste, and a roll of toilet paper wrapped in a plastic bag.

Tools — any piece of equipment used to help get something done. There are many specialized backpacking tools.

Topographical maps — maps which show the shape and make-up of the land. See *U.S. Geological Survey*.

Toxic — poisonous. Something toxic is harmful and sometimes can even kill. Know which snakes, animals and plants can transmit toxic substances.

Trail — a well-travelled path or a path which gets you where you want to go.

Trail blazing — see *breaking trail.*

Trail etiquette — how to act and stay healthy on the trail. Don't do anything which would reflect badly on you or others as hikers and human beings. Do not damage anything. Don't kick or throw rocks. Keep your garbage to yourself. Leave all living things to go about their business.

Trail head — the beginning of the trail.

Trail maps — maps which show which way to go. See *guidebook*.

Trail markers — signs which show you which trail goes in which direction. Markers often also indicate the degree of difficulty of hiking on that trail. They are usually found mounted on trees or posts at trail intersections or along long stretches of trail to confirm that you are going the right way. Ask about the trail markers in the area you'll be hiking and find out how to read them.

Trail snacks — light foods eaten during a short rest on the trail. Every few hours during your hike, stop to drink water and have a snack. This will help replace lost body energy. Trail snacks include raisins, health food candy bars, nuts, dried fruits, etc. Keep trail snacks in an easy-to-get-to outside pocket of your pack.

Trespassing — walking or standing around on property belonging to someone who does not want you there. When you go hiking or camping, make sure you're not trespassing.

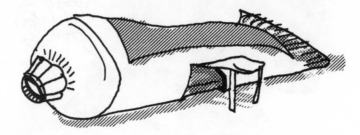

Tube tent — a tent made from a large piece of lightweight material and shaped like a wide tube, open at each end. This is a good choice for one person hiking in warm, stable weather. The roof is made by running a rope through the tube and tying the rope to trees. The weight of your body and supplies hold the floor down.

Tubular frame — a backpack frame made of hollow, tube-like sections, invented just before World War II. The frame is constructed with lightweight steel or aluminum. Joints in the frame should be welded, not bolted. See *frame, external frame* and *internal frame*.

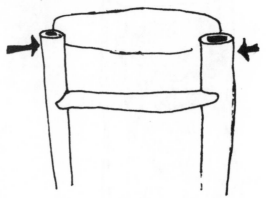

U

U.S. Forest Service — a government service which can give you information about rules and regulations in U.S. National Parks and Forests. Write to:

U.S. Forest Service
c/o U.S. Department of Agriculture
Washington, D.C. 20250

U.S. Geological Survey — a government service which can provide you with topographical maps for your expedition. Write to:

U.S. Geological Survey
12201 Sunrise Valley Drive
Reston, VA 22092

See *topographical maps.*

U.S. National Climatic Center — a national organization that provides weather information. If you're planning an outing in another state, contact them for weather predictions.

U.S. National Parks Service — a government service which can give you information about rules and regulations in U.S. National Parks and Forests. Write to:

> U.S. National Parks Service
> c/o U.S. Department of Interior
> Washington, D.C. 20240

Ultraviolet light — very hot light from the sun which you cannot see. When hiking at high altitudes, your skin gets more ultraviolet light and it can burn quickly, so cover up!

Underbrush — dense, low vegetation.

Underclothing — clothing worn under your shirt and pants. Wool or a blend of wool and cotton is the best material for a hiker's underclothes: you'll stay cool in summer and warm in winter.

Untamed — see *wild*.

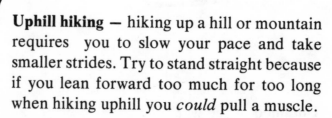

Uphill hiking — hiking up a hill or mountain requires you to slow your pace and take smaller strides. Try to stand straight because if you lean forward too much for too long when hiking uphill you *could* pull a muscle.

118

V

Vegetation — anything which grows out of the soil: plant life. Areas of dense vegetation are difficult to hike through if there are no established paths.

Ventilation — a system or situation in which fresh air replaces stale air: air circulation. Most good backpacks allow for ventilation between your back and the pack's material so your back won't sweat. Your tent should also have good ventilation (air vents). Make sure all air vents are kept clear.

Vest — a jacket without sleeves! Down vests are warmest.

Virgin forest — a forest untouched, unexplored or undeveloped by mankind.

W

Waist belt — a belt, attached to the external frame or the pack material, which transfers most of the weight of the load from your shoulders to your hips. The belt should be adjusted moderately snug at first. Then, after moving the pack higher up, the belt should be pulled nice and tight. A tight waist belt will provide better stability so you can keep your balance.

Waist pack — a mini-pack which is strapped around your waist. Good for a short hike, it can carry binoculars or camera equipment, and some trail snacks.

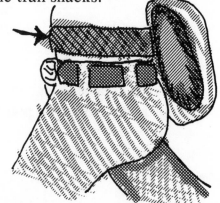

120

Waterfall — a natural formation of the land where water spills over the side of rocks or a mountain and falls, sometimes from great heights, crashing into water at the bottom. Niagara Falls and Yosemite Falls are both spectacular. Waterfalls are beautiful, but they can be dangerous.

Waterproof — anything that will not let water through. Waterproof material is necessary for your ground sheet and rainfly. Tent material (except the tent floor) and sleeping bag material should not be waterproof because the material will not be able to "breathe."

Water purification tablets — tablets that purify (cleanse) unsafe water. Add them to water from any untested supply which you are unsure of. Always bring a few along. If you're stuck without any and *must* drink suspicious water, boil the water thoroughly before drinking.

Water repellent — material which sheds water. The ability to repel water is not 100% with this type of material, but it has the advantage of being able to "breathe." See *breathable* and *sleeping bag*.

Weather — all the natural forces and conditions which make up the atmosphere. Weather is always a factor in planning and enjoying any backpacking trip. See *climate, the elements* and *temperature*.

Weight — how heavy something is. Always think of an object's weight before deciding to carry it with you into the woods. See *equilibrium* and *the load*.

Wet — covered with or saturated with water. When you are out hiking, try not to get wet, and keep water off your equipment and supplies. Remember, things have ways of getting wet besides getting rained on. See *dew*.

Whistle — a small device which, when blown into, produces a shrill, high-pitched sound. It's loud and it's a great aid if you get lost or need help. See *distress signal*.

White gas — a fuel for your cook-stove. A white gas flame is quick and clean, and the stove is excellent and easy to control, although sometimes a bit hard to start. White gas should be kept in a leak-proof, metal container which has a screw cap. Take along a pour spout. As always with gas fuel, be careful! See *pour spout*.

Wild — any living creature which is not tamed by man. Wild animals can be very unpredictable and can be dangerous if startled, provoked or hungry. Don't play with wild animals; observe them. Don't feed them. Feeding wild animals helps no one, and it is often dangerous.

Wilderness — untamed, uncultivated, undeveloped land. In the wilderness, animals live without man-made barriers and interference. An attraction to the wilderness is one thing that makes us want to go back-packing.

Wilderness area — an area protected and controlled by some authority in order to preserve the area's wildlife. Get permission before hiking and camping in a wilderness area, and know the rules and regulations. Sometimes one of the rules may be, "No Hiking or Camping!" See *trespassing*.

Wildlife — all untamed life in the wild. *We* were once wildlife! A hike into the wilderness is a little like going home.

Windbreak — anything which provides shelter from the wind: a wind barrier. It is a good idea to choose a campsite which has a natural windbreak, like a grove of trees, the side of a hill, etc. See *fire ring, shelter* and *windbreaker*.

Windbreaker — a lightweight jacket used to keep the wind off you.

Woods — an area of land covered with lots of trees. Don't wander far into the woods without being prepared! See *forest*.

Wool — a fabric made from the hair of sheep. It's excellent for hiking clothes. Wool keeps you cooler than synthetic materials in the summer, and warmer than almost any other material in the winter.

Y

Y-stakes — two stakes pushed into the ground on each side of an open fire. A green branch is then supported in the *V* of each stake. Food can then be hung from this green branch for cooking purposes. See *stakes*.

Z

Zipper — zippers are made of plastic or metal. Plastic zippers with large teeth are best because they won't jam as easily as metal zippers and tend not to freeze (a common problem with metal zippers under very cold conditions).

ABOUT THE AUTHOR

Randy Larson was born in New Brunswick, New Jersey. He has backpacked throughout the United States and Canada and has fought mountain forest fires in British Columbia, Canada. Mr. Larson holds degrees in philosophy, English literature and creative writing. He taught creative writing at the University of Colorado and has published much of his writing under another name. Currently living in Boston, Massachusetts, he is writing and working as a legal assistant in a law firm.

ABOUT THE ILLUSTRATOR

Eric Lurio earned his bachelor's degree from George Washington University and also attended Pratt Institute and the School of Visual Arts in New York City. He has lived in the New York City area most of his life. In addition to being an illustrator, he has also worked as a taxi driver, security guard, messenger and animator.